W9-CBU-222

YOUR SEXUAL HEALTH™

HIV/AIDS

KATHY FURGANG

ROSEN PUBLISHING®

New York

Published in 2016 by The Rosen Publishing Group, Inc.
29 East 21st Street, New York, NY 10010

Copyright © 2016 by The Rosen Publishing Group, Inc.

First Edition

Library of Congress Cataloging-in-Publication Data

Furgang, Kathy.
HIV/AIDS/Kathy Furgang.—First edition.
    pages cm.—Your sexual health)
Includes bibliographical references and index.
ISBN 978-1-4994-6066-7 (library bound)—ISBN 978-1-4994-6067-4 (paperback)—
ISBN 978-1-4994-6068-1 (6-pack)
1. HIV (Viruses)—Popular works. 2. AIDS (Disease)—Popular works. I. Title.
QR414.6.H58F87 2016
614.5'99392—dc23

        2014042047

For many of the images in this book, the people photographed are models. The depictions do not imply actual situations or events

Manufactured in the United States of America

CONTENTS

O f all the sexually transmitted diseases, HIV/AIDS has the reputation
of being the most frightening, the
most serious, and the deadliest. People
have that impression of the disease for a
good reason. HIV/AIDS has been a global
health issue since its emergence in the
early 1980s. Since then, the disease has
claimed more than thirty-nine million
lives around the globe.

We have learned many things about
HIV/AIDS since it was first discovered.
After the first epidemic and public
scares in the 1980s, we now know how
to take steps to manage the disease.
We've learned how this sexually transmitted disease (STD) spreads, how it can
be prevented, and whom it affects. The
early idea that HIV/AIDS is exclusively a
disease of gay men has been dispelled.
People have become more educated and
socially aware over the years. We now
know that the disease does not just
affect homosexuals and that a diagnosis
of HIV is not necessarily a death sentence. Although the disease has no cure,

The red ribbon is the symbol of HIV/AIDS prevention and awareness. This demonstration on World AIDS Day was held in Seoul, South Korea.

it is possible for many people today to have access to and respond successfully to medications that allow them to live active lives for decades. After years of learning about the disease, treating it, and educating the public, HIV/AIDS has come under control in many parts of the world.

Despite how far we've come in combatting the HIV/AIDS epidemic, the disease is still a powerful killer. About two million new cases are diagnosed annually.

In 2013 alone, approximately 1.5 million people around the world died from HIV-related diseases.

Today, about 70 percent of the new HIV infections are of people in sub-Saharan Africa. Nearly twenty-five million people in that region live with HIV. One reason for the concentration of people in that area is the lack of resources to help combat the disease. The easy access to medications we have in North America and in other first-world countries has not reached some of these regions.

Even though the majority of new HIV/AIDS cases occur in Africa, it would be a mistake for us to think that the disease is now a faraway problem. Today, one of the greatest dangers is letting our guard down about how to avoid contracting HIV/AIDS. Responsible sexual behavior has helped to curb the spread of the disease, but not continuing those efforts could cause its effects to spike out of control.

In addition, we can't rest or become complacent if the disease still persists in one part of the world. If the virus is still a problem for some areas, then it has the potential to be a problem everywhere.

Keeping up on education and public awareness is also important. New generations of sexually active people must learn about the risks of the disease and how to avoid it. By learning as much as we can about HIV/AIDS and how it affects the body, we may someday be able to find a cure and combat the disease for good.

CHAPTER ONE

What Is HIV/AIDS?

To understand one of the most feared diseases in modern history, let's begin by understanding what the acronym HIV/AIDS stands for. HIV stands for "human immunodeficiency virus." It is a virus whose last stage is called AIDS, or "acquired immunodeficiency syndrome." HIV is a virus that spreads from person to person, through bodily fluids such as semen and blood. HIV damages the immune system and makes the body less able to fight off other diseases. Imagine your body's defenses unable to fight off a cold or other illness. For people with HIV, simple illnesses are much more serious because the body does not fight off germs, bacteria, or other viruses like a healthy body would.

It is important to understand the difference between HIV and AIDS. Even though a person with HIV is at risk for getting seriously ill, he or she could live with the virus for many years without progressing to AIDS. The immune system will slowly weaken with HIV. A person is considered to have AIDS only after the immune system has weakened to a certain point. It is important to note that as soon as a person contracts HIV, he or she is infectious and can transmit the disease to others. Even though a person does not have AIDS, the disease that can ultimately cause AIDS can be transmitted from person to person.

HIV/AIDS attacks and destroys a type of white blood cell in the body called a CD4 cell, also known as a T cell. These are the cells that help the body fight off diseases. In a way,

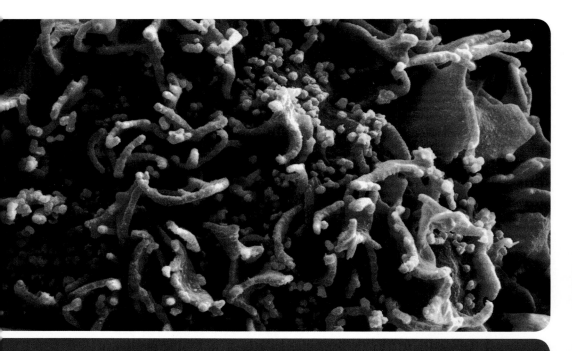

This scanning electron microscope image shows the HIV virus (in yellow) attacking a type of human white blood cell called a T cell.

HIV/AIDS is an illness of the immune system, which is meant to protect us and keep us healthy. A person with HIV will be monitored by doctors and have blood work checked regularly. When a person's CD4 cell count drops below two hundred, the person's illness is said to have progressed, and he or she is diagnosed with AIDS. A person with HIV can also be diagnosed with AIDS if he or she develops an illness that attacks and damages the immune system, no matter what his or her CD4 count is. These illnesses, called opportunistic infections, have a serious effect on an HIV patient's health. Tuberculosis (TB), pneumonia, salmonella, and herpes are examples of opportunistic infections. Opportunistic infections are the leading cause of death among HIV/AIDS patients.

HOW HIV/AIDS IS CONTRACTED

The HIV virus began in animal populations—possibly the monkey or chimp populations of Africa—and then passed to humans. A human might have contracted the disease after making contact with the animal's blood when it was hunted or cooked.

HIV is passed among humans through contact with bodily fluids, such as semen or vaginal secretions during sexual contact. It does not spread by touching other people, or even through saliva, as many people thought when the disease was first beginning to spread during the 1980s. The only way to contract the disease through saliva or by kissing someone is if one person has cuts, open sores, or bleeding gums, and blood is passed to the other person.

Sexual activity is not the only way HIV is passed. Blood transfusions are also one way in which the disease can be passed from person to person. Sharing needles or other drug paraphernalia is also a way to pass bodily fluids from one person to another and spread the disease.

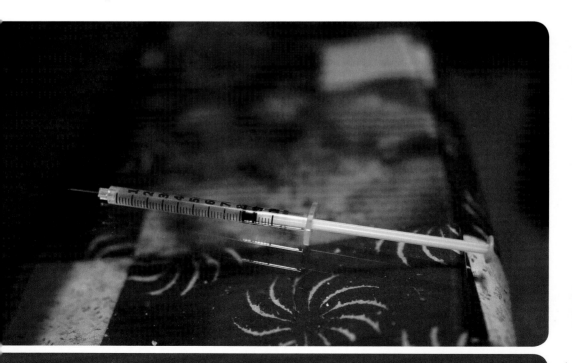

HIV/AIDS is spread through bodily fluids, which can be passed from one person to another when people share needles.

A mother can also pass the disease to her child when it is in the womb, during a vaginal delivery, or through breastfeeding.

SYMPTOMS AND PHASES OF THE DISEASE

The first signs of an HIV infection often come within two to four weeks after the person has been exposed. The symptoms are similar to the flu. A person may have a fever, diarrhea, headache, or muscle ache. Other symptoms include rashes, chills, sore throat, swollen glands, and joint pain. Open sores in the mouth or on the genitals, called ulcers, are also possible signs of the virus.

This first stage is sometimes called a primary HIV infection, and the stage may last anywhere from a few weeks to a few months. Many people describe this phase as being like a very bad flu. However, not all people experience this stage exactly the same way. For some, the symptoms may be so mild that a person will not notice them or feel they are enough to cause alarm. It is during this stage of active symptoms—regardless of their severity—that a person is producing the virus rapidly and is most capable of spreading the virus to others. As the virus is being produced in the body, a person's level of CD4 cells decreases. That's because the virus uses CD4 cells to reproduce and destroys the CD4 cells as it does so.

One of the most problematic aspects of the HIV virus is how difficult it is to determine whether someone has it in its initial phases. The virus cannot be detected through blood tests until several months after the infection. That means that a negative blood test—one in which the virus is not detected—does not necessarily mean that a person does not have HIV. It may take up to a couple months for a blood test to indicate that the virus is present. During that time, the person is very contagious and can more easily spread the disease than at other stages of the disease.

The only way a person can be sure that he or she is not passing the disease after a possible exposure is to abstain from unprotected sex and avoid other possible methods of transmission for months before taking a blood test.

Another difficult aspect of the disease is that the symptoms of the primary HIV infection are so similar to other diseases that they just seem like the flu or other less serious illnesses. A person would have to visit a doctor and get a special blood test to get a diagnosis of HIV.

After the primary HIV infection stage, the infection enters a latent stage. The virus is present in the body but reproducing at a slower rate. A person may not have any symptoms during this period. Without treatment, this stage lasts an average of ten years before progressing to AIDS, but some individuals may progress to AIDS much faster than others. With treatment, the clinical latency period can last

WHEN TO SEE A DOCTOR

If you feel you may have been exposed to HIV, it's time to see a doctor and find out. Even if you are not exhibiting the symptoms of a primary infection, it helps to get in touch with a doctor who might be able to monitor you. That way, the doctor can help you decide when the best time to test your blood might be and what to do if you start exhibiting active symptoms. The doctor will likely question you about how you may have come in contact with the disease. Be honest about your sexual activity or any other actions that might have put you in contact with the disease. Ask questions, and try to get informed about the disease. If you do have it, you'll be relieved to be under a doctor's care. If you don't have it, you will be relieved that you took steps to take care of your health and the health of your sexual partner.

several decades with no symptoms and no progression to AIDS.

Once a person has progressed to the stage of being diagnosed with AIDS, he or she can live up to three years but may die sooner. Treatment can help prolong an AIDS patient's life, but there is not yet a known cure for the disease. The most life-threatening part of HIV/AIDS is the likelihood of developing other fatal diseases due to a weakened immune system.

PEOPLE MOST AT RISK

During the first HIV/AIDS epidemic, in the 1980s, the homosexual community in the United States was hit the hardest. Because of this, people thought that the disease affected only gay men and anyone who had sexual contact with men who have sex with other men. While homosexual populations were at greatest risk in the 1980s because of the course of sexual exposure and contact, anyone can contract the disease.

Today, we might say that people from Africa are most at risk because that is where 70 percent of the new cases are being diagnosed. However, keep in mind that everyone has the potential of contracting the disease if proper precautions are not taken to prevent it. That means that people who have sex without a condom are at risk. Doing anything that provides the virus with an entry into blood or semen is considered risky

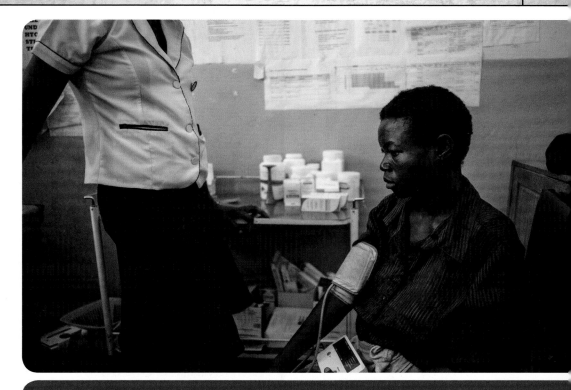

Health clinics in Africa, like this one in Malawi, treat a large number of new HIV/AIDS cases each year.

behavior. In turn, this behavior puts sexual partners at risk of contracting the disease as well. People who have open sores on their mouths or genitals produced by other STDs are also particularly at risk. These diseases include herpes, genital warts, and syphilis.

In addition, people who use needles or syringes are at risk of spreading the disease. Contaminated needles from drug use or transfusion provide an open passage for the virus into the body.

COMPLICATIONS

While the HIV/AIDS virus can be harmful and fatal to the body, the complications of the disease are often the reason that infected individuals do not live out the ten-year life expectancy of the disease. Instead of simply living an average of ten years with the disease without treatment, a patient whose CD4 levels have been lowered to a dangerous level is at greater risk of contracting a whole host of other life-threatening diseases that may result in an even shorter life expectancy. Tuberculosis is one of the most common complications for a weakened immune system.

Other common opportunistic infections include pneumonia, herpes, and candidiasis, also known as thrush. There are opportunistic cancers as well, the most common of which is Kaposi's sarcoma, a cancer that causes lesions on the skin.

MYTHS AND FACTS

MYTH
I do not have to use a condom if my partner tested negative for the HIV/AIDS virus.

FACT
The virus does not show up in blood tests for months after a person's contact with the disease. A person who tested negative may test positive days, weeks, or months later. Regular and proper use of condoms and other prophylactics during sexual activity will help prevent the spread of HIV/AIDS and other STDs.

MYTH
Someone who gets HIV/AIDS will likely die soon.

FACT
With treatment, a person can live an active life with HIV for decades.

MYTH
I cannot get HIV/AIDS by having sex with a virgin.

FACT
A virgin can contract HIV through oral sex or through nonsexual means, such as blood transfusions or sharing needles.

CHAPTER TWO

The Evolution of HIV/AIDS

The AIDS virus seemed to appear suddenly and spread quickly in the early 1980s. Men in gay communities in New York and Los Angeles began showing symptoms of odd infections, the rare cancer Kaposi's sarcoma, and signs of very weakened immune systems. It was not until 1982 that the disease was officially named AIDS, and it took even longer to understand that HIV is a separate virus that eventually causes AIDS.

During this time, a stigma arose about the disease's connection to the gay community. It even became known as the gay plague because of its disproportionate effect on the gay community. It was several years before an understanding arose that blood transfusions and intravenous drug use could also cause HIV/AIDS. Doctors began seeing the first cases of AIDS in infants who had had blood transfusions, as well as AIDS in newborns born to mothers with the virus.

The earliest cases of AIDS were analyzed by the Centers for Disease Control. AIDS research began in the early 1980s, soon after the first outbreak.

Cases of the disease spread quickly throughout North America and the rest of the world. The Centers for Disease Control (CDC) enacted procedures to help deal with the outbreak. The first hospital wards dedicated to treating the disease filled immediately with new patients, and guidelines were put in place about how health care workers would treat patients without becoming infected. This included the use of rubber gloves when touching patients' blood or bodily fluids, a practice that had not been routinely practiced before outside of the operating room.

The spread of the disease happened quickly because scientists were still learning about how the disease was contracted and when it could be passed to others. It was not until 1985 that a blood test to diagnose the disease was created. In addition to screening patients for the virus, the test was used by blood banks to ensure that blood donations were safe. This was one of the first steps in being able to stop the spread of the disease.

AIDS PANIC AND FEAR

The more widespread the outbreak of AIDS became in the 1980s, the more fear and panic grew among the general population. People became afraid of catching the disease because the details about how it was transmitted were discovered slowly. It was first thought that the disease could be spread through saliva, so kissing became a concern. People became afraid that the disease could be spread through any kind of sexual contact. Fear grew because the disease was so new and there was still a lot to learn about it.

People even became concerned about the disease spreading through all kinds of casual contact, including shaking hands. People who were diagnosed with HIV not only had to cope with the diagnosis, they also had to deal with the stigma of the disease among the general public. Many people feared HIV patients. It was nearly impossible for them to live normal lives.

Many people did not want to be around anyone who was gay, out of fear that they might have the disease. People who contracted the disease through blood transfusions were sometimes discriminated against and presumed to be homosexual. Such misunderstandings were common at the time and added to the chaos of the initial epidemic. People felt uncomfortable even talking about the disease because it was often sexually transmitted.

The fear and panic continued to spread because the number of cases continued to rise, and no known cure existed. Early medicines to treat the disease were ineffective and did not help much in prolonging patients' lives.

In 1985, a Hollywood icon of the 1950s and 1960s, Rock Hudson, died of AIDS. This shocked the world because it showed how widespread and far-reaching the disease had become so quickly. The death of Hudson and other well-known people—including tennis player Arthur Ashe—created support and concern among the population and helped encourage the government to research and combat the disease. The later revelation in 1991 that basketball star Magic Johnson was HIV positive brought the reality that anyone could contract the virus even further home for many Americans.

The first major public address on the disease by the president of the United States was made in 1987 by President Ronald Reagan. He vowed to make HIV/AIDS research and education a priority. As part of that effort, the government urged parents and schools to begin open lines of communication about AIDS, and the use of condoms was encouraged as a way to avoid the

RYAN WHITE

In 1984, thirteen-year-old Ryan White from Indiana contracted HIV through a blood transfusion, which he needed to treat his hemophilia, a blood disease. As a result, his middle school refused to allow him to attend out of fear for the other students. Parents did not want their children exposed to Ryan, and teachers felt uncomfortable dealing with the social issues that would arise because of the stigma of the disease. The situation represented the discrimination HIV patients experienced because of their disease. Ryan White was an important figure in the fight against AIDS discrimination. He spoke out against his treatment by his community and worked to educate people about the disease. He died in 1990 at age eighteen.

transmission of the disease. Although many Americans felt uncomfortable talking to their children about the issue, it was an important topic that needed to be addressed to help control the spread of the disease. Billions of dollars were invested in the research. The fight against AIDS came into the forefront of the American mind. In 1987, the U.S. Public Health Service (PHS) added AIDS to the list of dangerous contagious diseases that would prevent people from traveling or immigrating to the United States. The ban was not lifted until 1990.

By 1989, the number of reported AIDS cases in the United States hit one hundred thousand.

AIDS ACTIVISM

The AIDS crisis of the 1980s met with difficult obstacles in terms of prejudice, fear, and discrimination. This created a need for activism to help address these issues so that AIDS patients could get the help they needed and live their lives without unfair treatment.

The fact that the majority of people affected by the disease were gay men and drug users caused some people to view the disease as a moral punishment for unconventional behaviors and lifestyles. Compassion for the patient was often not considered until AIDS activism challenged these viewpoints and fought the disease through education, rather than ostracism of the patients.

The first AIDS activists rejected the portrayal of AIDS patients as victims of a lifestyle disease and began to get people living with AIDS involved in speaking to the public about the importance of addressing the public health issue. This allowed people to make a connection with people living with HIV/AIDS and understand that many are making an effort to live normal lives, hold jobs, and be part of society.

Organizations such as the AIDS Coalition to Unleash Power (ACT UP) started in 1987 with the goal of helping to bring awareness and understanding about the AIDS epidemic to the forefront for Americans. This group encouraged

The political activist group ACT UP has worked to make Americans aware of the AIDS epidemic in America since the late 1980s.

open dialogue about the disease and how it is spread in an effort to educate people. Its slogan Silence = Death conveyed the importance of educating and communicating about the disease. It sought to fight ignorance about how the disease is spread. It brought attention to the policies that showed fear and ignorance, such as the travel ban for people with HIV. ACT UP saw the AIDS epidemic as a political crisis in which the government was not doing as much as it could to fight the disease because of the stigma that was attached to it.

AIDS activists also helped bring attention to the problem by holding large-scale public memorials to honor those who had died of AIDS. For example, they encouraged candlelight vigils and the assembly of a huge AIDS memorial quilt, made from panels sewn by the relatives of people who have died of AIDS. This showed a more human side to the disease and its impact on society as a whole. People wishing to show support for the fight against AIDS could wear a red ribbon, often as a pin. This practice was derived from old customs of wearing ribbons during times of mourning.

AIDS activists also contributed a great deal to the push for development of medicines and therapies for the treatment of the disease. Political pressure placed on pharmaceutical companies by activist groups helped to accelerate the development of life-saving drugs. They made people aware of the urgency of

The AIDS Memorial Quilt—shown here on the National Mall in Washington, D.C.— personalized the AIDS struggle for many Americans living with the disease.

the need for many of these medicines and helped fight social indifference about the disease. Activists rallied the general public and gained a lot of support for their efforts to force the government and corporations to action.

POSITIVE STEPS

AIDS activism in the 1980s and 1990s helped to bring education to the forefront. The sexual revolution of the 1960s and 1970s resulted in many more people having sex with multiple partners. The introduction of the birth control pill also gave women increased sexual freedom with less worry about becoming pregnant. The use of condoms was not widespread, however, until sexually transmitted diseases such as HIV/AIDS became widespread. The AIDS epidemic and AIDS activism made "safe sex" a mainstream concept. This was a positive step in helping to promote sexual health among both the homosexual and hetero-sexual populations.

The work of AIDS activists also helped to put pressure on state governments to make needle exchange programs legal. The 1980s were not only the time of the AIDS epidemic, but they were also the time that the United States' War on Drugs resulted in some of the

AIDS IN THE MEDIA

As the public learned more about the disease, a shift began to occur that focused more on the patient than the disease. Television, plays, and movies began to feature characters with HIV/AIDS, making the public more aware of their struggles. The 1993 film *Philadelphia*, staring Tom Hanks, was the first major Hollywood movie about the subject, and it was based on a true story. In 1993, the play *Angels in America* tackled the topic, winning a Tony Award for Best Play, as well as the Pulitzer Prize for Drama. As the epidemic in Africa grew, the South African version of the children's television show *Sesame Street* created an HIV-positive Muppet character named Kami. She helped to teach children about AIDS.

highest incarceration rates for drug-related crimes. Making needle exchange programs legal for illegal drug users was in direct opposition to the hard stance that the government was taking against drugs. However, public pressure and the work of AIDS activists helped many states decide to make the programs legal in the interest of public health.

The activism and education of the public also brought positive changes in the way the homosexual community was viewed. Once the public learned more about people in the gay community living with HIV, those people became more familiar and more accepted. While there was still a lot of opposition, improvements were being made.

The widespread testing for the HIV virus also helped educate young people about being responsible in their sexual activity. Not only were people having safe sex, but many were regularly getting tested for the HIV antibodies, for their own health and for the protection of their sexual partner.

CHAPTER THREE

HIV/AIDS Prevention

Education is the key to prevention. The more we know about how people become HIV positive and contract this incurable disease, the more we can do to prevent it from happening. Today, we have the benefit of a few decades of experience with the disease, so we know how it is transmitted and how to treat it. The preventative measures involved in curbing the spread of AIDS involve keeping open communication with partners, which can sometimes be difficult. But when you think about the importance of preventing one of the deadliest diseases of our times, communication problems seem like something that can be overcome. Behaving responsibly and keeping the lines of communication open between you and a partner can help prevent the spread of HIV/AIDS.

BEHAVIOR

The only way to truly stay safe from any STD—HIV/AIDS and others—is to practice abstinence. In addition to not wanting to contract an STD, many teens abstain from sexual contact because they are simply not ready for it. Communication with a partner about sex is important. Only become as sexually involved as you feel comfortable being. This will help you be emotionally ready for any challenges that may arise in your relationship. Remember that HIV is not transmitted through kissing unless one or both partners has an open sore or cut in the mouth.

Teens who are just starting to become sexually active and have not had multiple partners are indeed at a lower risk of contracting HIV, but it is still important to know how the disease is transmitted. Someone who obtained the virus through intravenous drug use can then spread it to others through sexual contact, even if that person has not been sexually active before.

The next best way to prevent the spread of HIV and other STDs is to practice safe sex. This means having protected sex by using a condom each and every time you have sex. Using a condom regularly and correctly is the only way in which a person can have sex without bodily fluids entering the partner's body.

Women who use birth control might think they are practicing safe sex because they are preventing pregnancy. However, that is not what safe sex means. Safe sex methods

prevent disease, not pregnancy. So a woman who uses birth control pills still needs to use a condom, dental dam, or other protection in order to practice safe sex with her partner.

The wide availability of condoms makes it easier to practice safe sex.

Practicing safe oral sex is also necessary to prevent the possibility of spreading HIV through sexual contact. Some couples try to avoid pregnancy by having oral sex. While oral sex does not cause pregnancy, it can cause STDs to spread. Preventing the exchange of bodily fluids during oral sex entails covering the genital being touched by the mouth. Latex barriers of various kinds are sold in stores.

If both partners have HIV/AIDS, they should use protection as well. Even though they already have the virus, there are different strains that could be passed back and forth. The protection would also keep them from getting other sexually transmitted diseases that would further damage their immune systems and become opportunistic infections.

Other ways to stay protected from the spread of HIV/AIDS include not sharing needles and avoiding contact with blood. All blood given for transfusions is now screened and should be free of infection. People do not need to worry about HIV/AIDS being transmitted through blood transfusions, but the sharing of needles is still a big concern because it could involve contact with an infected person's blood.

People who know they are at high risk for HIV from sexual activity or drug use can take steps to prevent a permanent infection. A pill called pre-exposure prophylaxis, or PrEP, can be taken every day to help prevent the virus from causing an infection. The pill is known as Truvada, and it contains two medicines that are part of an HIV drug treatment plan. If the pill is taken every day consistently, it can reduce a person's risk of getting HIV by up to 92 percent. The effectiveness of the pill is greatly reduced if the pill is not taken consistently. Using condoms in addition to a PrEP pill can provide even greater protection than just using the pill alone. According to the Centers for Disease Control and Prevention, people committed to taking the prescription drug should follow up with their care provider every three months. People considered to be at high risk and good candidates for the medicine include gay or bisexual men with partners at risk for exposure to the virus, people who inject drugs, or those whose partners inject drugs.

HEALTH CARE PROTECTION

HIV/AIDS is more than just a sexually transmitted disease. Contact with infected blood must also be avoided in order to stay safe from the disease. Doctors and nurses come into contact with blood on a regular basis. In addition, patients could be infected if they come in contact with a cut or sore on an infected health care worker. In 1990, a Florida dentist transmitted HIV to six of his patients. While no one is entirely sure how the dentist spread the virus to them, the use of additional protective gear became commonplace. All health care workers take steps to protect themselves against the blood of patients. Emergency-room workers will often wear gloves and other protective gear to help protect themselves from patients with unknown or undiagnosed illnesses, including HIV/AIDS.

COMMUNICATION

People must take on the task of staying safe from HIV by communicating with their partners. Knowing if your partner is at high risk means knowing about that person's sexual history. When considering sex with a new partner, or even when you are in a committed relationship, it is important to talk openly and honestly about the possibility of any sexually transmitted diseases. This will inform you and your partner about any risks for any sexually transmitted disease, not just for HIV/AIDS. Be open and honest about your own sexual history. That does not mean giving up your privacy completely and telling your partner about every person you dated. You are entitled to keep your private life private. However, be honest about whether your history could put someone at risk. Unprotected sex puts both you and your

Open and honest communication is needed when new partners discuss their sexual history.

partner at risk, even when neither of you have had many partners.

Communication about sexual history can be a potential sore spot for couples. One person may wish to keep his or her past sexual activity private, and that should be respected. A general idea about whether the person is at high risk should be enough for the partner to take the necessary precautions and possibly get tested for HIV.

It may be a good idea for two new partners to agree to get HIV blood tests before engaging in any sexual activity. This may seem overly cautious, but it could help protect the people involved, especially if they are not ready to share private information about their past.

GETTING TESTED

If you feel you may have been exposed to HIV, it is important to get tested as soon as possible. There are a few different types of tests. The most common tests screen for antibodies—that is, proteins in the blood that are produced as a response to a foreign substance in the body, in this case, the HIV virus. Because it can take the body a couple of months to produce these antibodies, however, these tests can indicate no presence of the virus even though you may have been infected. While blood is usually drawn for these standard tests, saliva or urine may sometimes be tested. Another

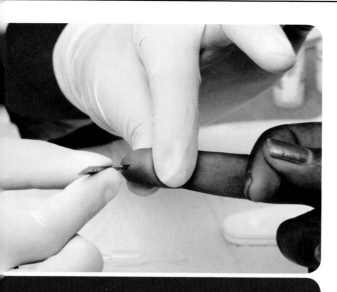

For a standard HIV test, blood is drawn and tested for the HIV antibody.

kind of test, called a rapid antibody test, can detect the HIV antibody in saliva, urine, or blood, and results can be provided in less than thirty minutes.

Antigen tests screen your blood for the presence of the HIV antigen, which is a protein specific to the virus. Standard blood tests check for these antigens and are sent out to laboratories for analysis. Though antibody tests are more common, the antigen test might result in an earlier diagnosis. The antigen test can detect HIV even one to three weeks after you first become infected. Fourth-generation tests require both antibody and antigen tests. These tests are more sensitive than either antibody or antigen tests alone and can result in an earlier HIV/AIDS diagnosis.

Other tests include the PCR test, which is typically used on babies who were born to HIV-positive mothers. This test can identify the genetic material of HIV as early as two to three weeks after infection.

Newer tests have been developed that can detect the virus in the body sooner than the standard test. The CDC recommends these tests because they can detect the virus up to four weeks earlier. This can inform the patient sooner allowing treatment to start earlier and keeping the patient from infecting other people.

The Affordable Care Act now requires that HIV screenings be covered by health insurance without a co-pay. People without health insurance can check the National HIV and STD Testing Resources section of the CDC website and enter their zip code for a list of places that provide HIV screenings for free or for a reduced cost.

Home tests are also available for people to buy at drug stores. In one kind of test, a person provides a small sample of his or her blood and sends it to a lab for testing. After three business days, the results can be given over the phone. The patient may remain anonymous when taking part in the test. The other kind of home test involves taking a swab of saliva from the mouth and putting it into a vial that will develop the results at home in up to forty minutes. Anyone receiving positive results from a home test must consult a doctor for further care and treatment. As with other tests, a negative result may not necessarily mean that you are not infected. A follow-up test or doctor visit is recommended.

10 GREAT QUESTIONS
TO ASK A DOCTOR ABOUT HIV/AIDS

1. What should I do if my partner does not want to practice safe sex?

2. Does my partner have the right to know whom I have had sexual contact with?

3. What should I do if my partner tells me he or she has a sexually transmitted disease?

4. What type of HIV test should I get?

5. What precautions must I take in order to live safely with HIV among my family members?

6. What should I do if my HIV test is positive?

7. Who will pay for my HIV test?

8. Can I get opportunistic infections before I test positive for HIV?

9. What can an HIV-positive person do to keep from getting AIDS?

10. What will happen if I have a reaction to medications for HIV?

CHAPTER FOUR

Treatment Options

Although HIV and AIDS are diseases with no cure, there are a wide variety of treatments to combat the virus with high rates of success. Once a person is diagnosed with HIV, the virus that causes AIDS, the object is to keep the patient from having a CD4 count below two hundred and from getting an opportunistic infection.

There are many things to consider if you are diagnosed as having HIV. A good relationship with a doctor will be an important step toward taking care of yourself. Talk with your doctor and loved ones about how you could receive the best care. This might mean finding a treatment center that can handle your disease better than the doctor you are currently seeing. In other cases, your doctor may be able to help you manage the disease or have access to facilities that are experienced in HIV care. It is also important to consider health insurance

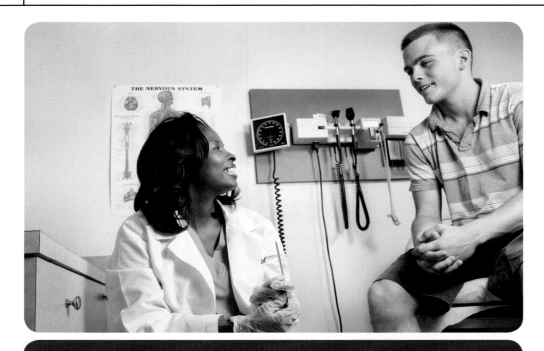

Having a trusted doctor can be one of the most important parts of an HIV or AIDS patient's treatment.

and the cost of the care you will receive. Work out these details with your family and your doctor. HIV requires regular monitoring by a trusted doctor, and the blood tests and screenings can go on for decades. Make sure you are satisfied with your health care provider and have an approved plan for your treatment.

GET INFORMED

One of the most important things to do if diagnosed with HIV is to be as informed as possible. It may be a frightening experience to be diagnosed with such a serious illness, but staying empowered and informed as a patient can help you manage your illness and monitor your progress. Don't let the disease paralyze you with fear. Finding out as much as possible about the disease will help you stay mentally equipped to deal with it.

For example, be familiar with the terms your doctor will be discussing with you. CD4 is a protein in your white blood cells that is attacked by HIV and destroyed by the virus. Doctors will monitor HIV by counting the levels of CD4 in your blood. That will show how much of the virus has taken over your system. A CD4 count for a healthy person is anywhere between five hundred and over one thousand. A person with a CD4 count from two hundred to five hundred is considered to be HIV positive. A person with a CD4 count below two hundred is considered to have AIDS, even if that person is feeling well and not exhibiting symptoms. The exception would be if a person with HIV develops an opportunistic infection, such as tuberculosis, pneumonia, or cancer. In that case, the HIV patient's diagnosis would progress to AIDS, regardless of his or her CD4 count.

Remember that a person who is receiving the best available care, exhibiting no symptoms, and measuring a relatively high CD4 count is still contagious and can spread the disease to others. The care and attention to the disease must not diminish, for the sake of the patient as well as those the person is in contact with. Inform any new health care workers you encounter that you are HIV positive so they can take the correct protective measures in caring for you. You may come across a wide variety of health care workers who draw your blood or care for you during your time receiving HIV care. Make sure they are informed about your HIV status.

Before HIV treatment is begun, a patient will have a complete review of his or her medical history with a doctor. Any medications a person takes already can affect the way HIV medications work in the body. Monitoring for new infections is also necessary. This is why

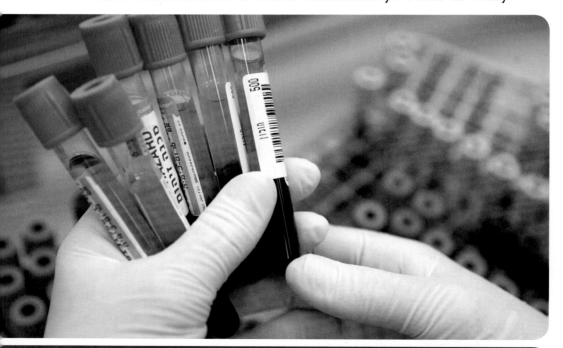

Any health care worker handling blood samples should be informed if a patient has HIV/AIDS.

a good relationship with a doctor is essential for an HIV/AIDS patient.

HIV DRUGS

The first drug to treat AIDS, called AZT, was approved in 1987. Since then, about thirty more drugs have become available to HIV and AIDS patients. This is excellent news because it has been found that a combination of drugs is the most effective way to control the virus in the body.

Drugs that treat HIV are called antiretrovirals (ARVs). All ARVs are designed to prevent HIV from replicating in the body. There are five separate classes of ARVs, each with a different approach to dealing with the virus. Some are better suited to certain stages of the disease than others. For example, one type disables the protein that HIV uses to duplicate itself. Another type of drug blocks the virus from entering cells in the first place. As part of antiretroviral therapy (ART), patients are often given a combination of drugs from the different classes. This combination of drugs is also called a drug cocktail, or highly active antiretroviral therapy (HAART). If a patient has a bad reaction to one type of medication, another type can be given. If one type of medicine is not producing good results, another one might be more successful. The drug treatments are generally started when the CD4 count falls below 350.

Controlling and introducing changes to an HIV/AIDS patient's medications is extremely important for two reasons. One reason is that the body can develop resistance to medications after they have been take taken for a long period of time. That would mean that the medicine is no longer doing its job or helping the patient. This can lower CD4 levels and make the patient sicker. The second reason is that the long-term side effects of some of the medicines can be damaging to the patient's health. Short-term side effects of the medicines can include diarrhea, dizziness, fatigue, or headaches. However, long-term side effects can affect the patient's reaction to insulin and may even cause diabetes. In addition, bone density can be compromised, resulting in an increased chance of broken bones. Among the most serious side effects are liver failure. Keeping on top of the medications and how they are affecting the body is an important part of the care of an HIV-positive patient. Always communicate with your doctor about the effects you are experiencing in order to make sure that he or she can find the right balance of medications and dosages for you at any given stage of the disease.

The longer HIV is successfully kept under control, the longer it will take for a person's illness to progress to AIDS. People have been living active and fulfilling lives with the HIV virus for decades while being treated.

Every three to six months, an HIV patient's blood must be checked for his or her viral load. The viral load is the measure of how much of the HIV virus is in the blood. In addition to these screenings, the blood is tested for other substances that can tell how well body parts such as the kidneys and liver are working. These tests must also be performed after an initial diagnosis, before a patient

COMING A LONG WAY

In the late 1980s, the first and only drug to treat AIDS was AZT. Today HIV/AIDS research has come such a long way that patients have a wide variety of treatment options available to them. The difference between the success rate of today's drugs and those in the early days of the disease are vast. An antiretroviral medicine for HIV was even used to treat Ebola patients in western Africa after the 2014 outbreak of that disease. Doctors dealing with the Ebola outbreak have had success with the HIV medicine lamivudine. Although it has not been shown to work in 100 percent of cases, it has had some very positive results.

begins taking a new HIV medication, and after a patient has started a new medication. A close check must also be done to ensure that any opportunistic infection is caught and treated as soon as possible. Once a person is diagnosed with AIDS, any opportunistic infection must be aggressively treated.

HIV/AIDS AND PREGNANCY

Women with HIV should be aware that they can still have healthy babies who are free of HIV. A couple in which one or both partners are infected with the disease and who want to have a baby can consult a doctor to evaluate their options so that they do not have to risk having unprotected sex. Taking extra care in pregnancy and even before pregnancy can help a woman stay as

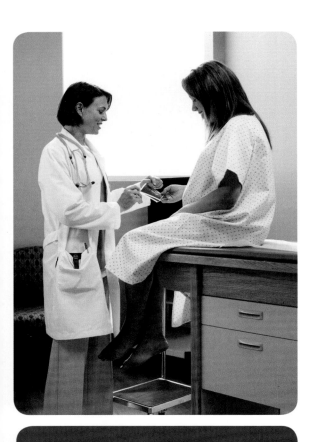

With the right care, women with HIV can still become pregnant and have a baby free of the disease.

healthy as possible. It is recommended that a pregnant woman take only certain types of HIV medications but that medications should definitely be taken to keep the mother's viral load and CD4 levels low. Because pregnancy can put a strain on the body, an HIV-positive woman should strive to be as healthy as possible before becoming pregnant. HIV-positive women who are or want to become pregnant should always consult a doctor for medical care specific to their needs.

Delivery of the child should also be done with special precaution because the baby is at risk of getting the virus during childbirth. A cesarean delivery is usually the best method for preventing the passage of bodily fluids from mother to child during delivery.

With the proper care, the risk of a mother passing HIV to her newborn is below 2 percent. The proper care involves getting the right drugs and having them at the correct time during pregnancy. Breastfeeding is not an option for HIV-positive mothers because nursing is one of the ways that the virus can be spread to a child. Just after a baby is born to an HIV-positive mother, the baby will be tested for the virus and a safe drug treatment can be administered, if needed.

CHAPTER FIVE

Living and Coping with HIV/AIDS

Receiving an HIV diagnosis can be devastating. Just as a patient should seek help immediately to help deal with the medical response to the illness, an emotional support team is also extremely important. Some people may need help talking to their loved ones about their diagnosis. Breaking the news to a partner or parents can be very difficult to do. Many people need counseling for how to speak to loved ones about what the diagnosis means for them. In some cases, parents or other loved ones may not know about a person's sexual history and may be shocked to learn about a diagnosis of HIV. Family counseling or couples counseling can be necessary for some patients.

SUPPORT GROUPS

There are support groups and peer groups that can help a patient or that person's family members to cope with the disease. In addition to the stress the disease may put on the patient, his or her caregivers may experience stress and need support as well. Some family members or caregivers of HIV patients may even have fears about the disease based on misinformation. Getting help for the whole network of people associated with the patient is important.

Support groups and counseling services are available for HIV patients and their partners and family members.

Counselors can also work one-on-one to deal with some of the emotions that go with having the virus. Some counselors specialize in treating people with HIV/AIDS. Get a recommendation from a doctor or leader of a support group about what kind of counselor might be right for your situation. People who seek the emotional help they need may be able to live a more peaceful or fulfilling life with the disease.

For people who feel uncomfortable seeking out support groups or counselors, online support is also available. In online support groups, people can read each other's stories, provide each other with support in preparing for an HIV test or dealing with a diagnosis, discuss treatments, and support each other if and when they feel ready to reach out to counselors in person.

Although HIV/AIDS is an extremely dangerous disease and can be fatal, life expectancy is very good for people diagnosed with the disease early—generally when their CD4 count is above 350. A healthy lifestyle is also a good indicator of life expectancy. A person who

Receiving support from close family and friends can help the mental health and overall well-being of an HIV/AIDS patient.

does not smoke, drink, or take other drugs while being treated for HIV will have a longer life expectancy as well. Included in a person's general health is mental health. Reaching out for emotional support can actually help a person's well-being. The rate of depression is twice as high among the HIV-positive population as it is among the general population, so reaching out for help is especially important. Not only will a patient receive care, but that patient can, in turn, provide support to others as well.

A WORD ABOUT ANIMALS

Animals can provide **HIV/AIDS** patients with some of the love and support they need to face their disease. However, make sure your animal sees a vet regularly. Living with animals can present unique challenges to people living with **HIV** or **AIDS**. Pets carry parasites or diseases that can affect the patient. Salmonella or other illnesses can interfere with a patient's battle to avoid infections.

DEALING WITH UNSUPPORTIVE PEOPLE

Despite all efforts to get support, some people are faced with unsupportive friends or family members. Overcoming these difficult situations is important for the overall health of the patient. That's where support groups can be helpful. Mending relationships with parents or friends who may have misconceptions is worth it so that the patient can live as normal a life as possible. Remember that a diagnosis may be very difficult for the family and friends as well as the patient. Family members may need time to adjust to the change in their lives. Taking the time to work out problems can be worth it for the patient, who should not have to face the problem alone. An HIV/AIDS diagnosis may even be shocking enough to break up the patient's relationship with his or her partner. It is normal to expect an adjustment period for people first learning the news of the diagnosis. But working through the problem together and even seeking counseling should then allow the patient to concentrate on his or her care. Being surrounded by supportive people is an important goal for an HIV or AIDS patient. Breaking off unhealthy relationships may be necessary in order to get that positive support team.

ACCENTUATE THE POSITIVE

The importance of positive thinking cannot be underestimated when dealing with any disease, not just HIV/AIDS. A person's emotional state can have a profound effect on his or her outlook on life and success with the disease. A positive outlook can also do wonders for other HIV patients and provide inspiration for their own battles.

PAYING ATTENTION TO HEALTH

Eating healthy foods and avoiding that which is unhealthy is important for keeping the body strong and healthy. Taking care of one's body is perhaps more important after an HIV or AIDS diagnosis than ever before. When the virus is in the body, it makes the immune system very susceptible to disease and infection. Even illnesses that are normally minor can become a major health problem for an HIV or AIDS patient.

Immunizations can be important for someone with HIV so that new illnesses are not introduced to the body. However, an HIV

A person diagnosed with HIV must maintain a healthy diet to keep the body working at its best.

patient must not have immunizations that contain live viruses. While a healthy body would fight off the live virus in an immunization, a person with HIV would be sickened and weakened by it.

Living as a teen with HIV can be especially challenging because peer pressure and social events can put the patient in contact with behaviors that would be particularly damaging. Smoking, drinking, or drug use would jeopardize the health of a young HIV patient even more than they would a nonaffected person. However, remember that HIV does not have to mean a social death sentence. Having information, proper medical care, and a group of supportive friends or family can help provide an HIV patient with lower-risk social interactions that can support a longer, more fulfilling, and healthier lifestyle.

GLOSSARY

abstinence The practice of restraining one-self from taking part in a particular activity, such as being sexually active.

AIDS Acquired immunedeficiency syndrome; a disease that attacks the body's ability to fight disease and infection by attacking the body's CD4, or T cells. It is the last stage of HIV infection.

antibody A blood protein that is produced in response to a specific bacteria, virus, or foreign substance in the blood.

antigen A foreign or harmful substance that, after entering the body, prompts the immune system to produce antibodies.

antiretroviral A drug that targets a particular type of virus called a retrovirus, such as HIV.

AZT Azidothymidine; an antiviral drug and the first medication available to treat HIV, the virus that causes AIDS.

CD4 A glycoprotein found on the cells (T cells) that help the body fight off disease; the type of cells attacked by the HIV virus.

condom Thin latex barrier worn on the penis during sexual intercourse to prevent infection and pregnancy.

drug cocktail A combination of drugs that fight a particular disease or infection.

epidemic A widespread occurrence of an infectious disease occurring in a population during a relatively short period of time.

heterosexual A person who is sexually attracted to people of the opposite sex.

HIV Human immunodeficiency virus; the virus that causes AIDS.

homosexual A person who is sexually attracted to people of the same sex.

immune system The parts of the body that respond to and fight off infection, disease, and toxins.

intravenous Inserted or administered into a human vein.

Kaposi's sarcoma A type of cancer common in AIDS patients, associated with lesions on the skin.

latent Lying hidden, or dormant, with no symptoms.

opportunistic infection Illnesses, such as tuberculosis, pneumonia, or Kaposi's sarcoma, that can attack someone with a weakened immune system and that have a particularly bad effect on the health of an HIV patient.

PrEP Pre-exposure phrophylaxis; a drug treatment that helps prevent HIV infection for people in high-risk populations.

prophylactic A medicine or procedure that helps prevent disease.

STD Sexually transmitted disease; examples include HIV/AIDS, herpes, and gonorrhea.

viral load A measurement of the amount of a virus in the bloodstream or body, usually measured in particles per milliliters.

FOR MORE INFORMATION

Advocates for Youth
2000 M Street NW, Suite 750
Washington, DC 20036
(202) 419-3420
Website: http://www.advocatesforyouth.org
Advocates for Youth helps young people make
    informed and responsible decisions about
    their sexual and reproductive health.

The AIDS Institute
1705 DeSales Street NW
Suite 700
Washington, DC 20036
(202) 835-8373
Website: http://www.theaidsinstitute.org
Through research, public policy, advocacy,
    and education initiatives, the AIDS Institute
    seeks to inform and act to prevent the fur-
    ther spread of HIV/AIDS.

Canadian AIDS Society (CAS)
190 O'Connor Street, Suite 100
Ottawa, ON K2P 2R3
Canada
(613) 230-3580
Website: http://www.cdnaids.ca
CAS acts on behalf of Canadians living with
    HIV/AIDS and community AIDS organiza-
    tions by educating and informing the public
    about the disease, promoting public policy
    at the national level, and mobilizing com-
    munities.

U.S. Department of Health and Human Services
Health Resources and Services Administration
    HIV/AIDS Bureau
5600 Fishers Lane
Rockville, MD 20857
(888) 275-4772
Website: http://hab.hrsa.gov
The organization administers the Ryan White
    HIV/AIDS Program, which provides local,
    city, and state HIV-related services.

World Health Organization (WHO)
20, Avenue Appia
CH-1211 Geneva 27
Switzerland
Website: http://www.who.int
WHO provides updated worldwide information
    about HIV/AIDS, as well as testing and coun-
    seling to help people cope with HIV/AIDS.

WEBSITES

Because of the changing nature of Internet
links, Rosen Publishing has developed an online list of websites related to the subject of
this book. This site is updated regularly. Please
use this link to access this list:

http://www.rosenlinks.com/YSH/HIV

FOR FURTHER READING

Fan, Hung Y., Ross F. Conner, and Luis P. Villar-real. *AIDS: Science and Society.* Sudbury, MA: Jones & Bartlett Learning, 2013.

Frazier, Joyce Marie. *Doing "It" Right: A Guide to Teen Sexuality.* Washington, DC: Y-Not Publishing, 2013.

Gallant, Joel E. *100 Questions & Answers About HIV and AIDS.* Sudbury, MA: Jones & Bartlett Learning, 2012.

Halkitis, Perry N. *The AIDS Generation: Stories of Survival and Resilience.* Oxford, England: Oxford University Press, 2013.

Harden, Victoria A. *AIDS at 30: A History.* Dulles, VA: Potomac Books, 2012.

Jones, Molly. *AIDS.* New York, NY: Rosen Publishing Group, 2011.

Marsico, Katie. *HIV/AIDS.* Edina, MN: ABDO Publishing, 2010.

Pepin, Jacques. *The Origins of AIDS.* Cambridge, England: Cambridge University Press, 2011.

Rocker, Chris. *HIV & Nutrition: Your Bible on Living with HIV/AIDS.* Seattle, WA: Amazon Digital Services, 2014.

Scannell, Kate. *Death of the Good Doctor: Lessons from the Heart of the AIDS Epidemic.* Seattle, WA: Create Space Independent Publishing Platform, 2012.

Simons, Rae. *A Kid's Guide to AIDS and HIV.* Vestal, NY: Village Earth Press, 2013.

BIBLIOGRAPHY

AIDS.org. "HIV Travel/Immigration Ban: Background, Documentation." Retrieved October 14, 2014 (http://www.aids.org/topics/hiv-travelimmigration-ban).

AIDS.gov. "Stages of HIV Infection." Retrieved October 15, 2014 (http://www.aids.gov/hiv-aids-basics/just-diagnosed-with-hiv-aids/hiv-in-your-body/stages-of-hiv).

Avert.org. "HIV Strains: Types, Groups, Subtypes." Retrieved October 14, 2014 (http://www.avert.org/hiv-types.htm).

Cancer.org. "Kaposi Sarcoma." Retrieved October 14, 2014 (http://www.cancer.org/cancer/kaposisarcoma/detailedguide/index).

Carter, Michael. "Mother-to-Baby Transmission." Aids Map, August 8, 2011. Retrieved October 17, 2014 (http://www.aidsmap.com/Mother-to-baby-transmission/page/1044918).

Centers for Disease Control and Prevention. "Testing." Retrieved October 15, 2014 (http://www.cdc.gov/hiv/basics/testing.html).

Cichocki, Mark. *Living with HIV: A Patient's Guide.* Jefferson, NC: McFarland, 2009.

Fetters, Ashley. "From Haight Street to Sesame Street: The Evolution of AIDS in Pop Culture." *Atlantic*, December 4, 2012. Retrieved October 17, 2014 (http://www.theatlantic.com/entertainment/archive/2012/12/from-haight-street-to-sesame-street-the-evolution-of-aids-in-pop-culture/265872).

Healthline Editorial Team. "HIV/AIDS Complications." September 8, 2011. Retrieved October

15, 2014 (http://www.healthline.com/health/
hiv-aids/complications#1).

Health Resources and Services Administration.
"Who Was Ryan White?" Retrieved October
15, 2014 (http://hab.hrsa.gov/abouthab
/ryanwhite.html).

Mayo Clinic Staff. "Diseases and Conditions:
HIV/AIDS." Mayo Clinic. Retrieved October
17, 2014 (http://www.mayoclinic.org/
diseases-conditions/hiv-aids/basics/
definition/con-20013732).

National Prevention Information Network.
"STDs." Retrieved October 15, 2014 (https://
npin.cdc.gov/disease/stds).

New York Public Library. "Why We Fight:
Remembering AIDS Activism." Retrieved
October 13, 2014 (http://www.nypl.org
/events/exhibitions/why-we-fight/more).

Palo Alto Medical Foundation. "Safer Oral Sex
Practices." October 14, 2014 (http://www
.pamf.org/teen/sex/std/oral).

WebMD. "Screening Tests for HIV Diagnosis
and Treatment." Retrieved October 14, 2014
(http://www.webmd.com/hiv-aids/hiv-aids
-screening).

INDEX

ABOUT THE AUTHOR

Kathy Furgang is an author who has written numerous educational books for teens. She has written on a variety of subjects, including careers, health, and other science topics. She also writes teacher guides and textbooks for students in elementary and middle school.

PHOTO CREDITS

Designer: Michael Moy; Editor: Shalini Saxena